Mastering the

MW01109924

Raymond J Roberge, MBA

&

Michael McIntyre, PhD

ISBN-10: 1977560563
ISBN-13: 978-1977560568

Acknowledgements:

They say it takes a village. In the case of this book, that certainly holds true. Without the help and support of many people, this collaboration could have never happened. Both of us would like to thank our colleagues, our students and our fellow executives, who have shaped our leadership styles.

To our readers, we thank you for allowing us to share our insights and hope you find them helpful in your quest for leadership excellence!

CONTENTS

1
WHAT IS LEADERSHIP?

Ask ten people the definition of leadership, and you'll get ten different answers. For the purpose of this book, leadership means *influencing a group of people to drive positive results*. It's important to note that we use the term *influencing* and not the term *directing*. It's easy for people in authority positions, like supervisors and managers, to play the power card, barking out commands and demanding obedience. But whether you care to admit it or not, that really amounts to threatening people–"Do what I say, or bad things will happen to you," and people don't respond well to threats. There's an old adage that says, "Every act of aggression is met with some form of retaliation," and that applies here. If you play the power card too often, you'll eventually start having problems with theft, absenteeism, shoddy work and accidents. And, if the economy is good and team members are feeling mobile, you'll also face employee turnover.

Leadership is about getting people to *want* to be productive. It's about building people's sense of personal ownership and commitment. If you lead people effectively, they'll have a positive effect on the business, because they'll embrace the mission. If you lead people effectively, they'll continue to create positive outcomes, even when you're not around.

Most leaders are action-oriented people who like solving problems and enjoy the adrenaline rush of being in the trenches. But a good leader needs to carve out some time to think about the business, reflect on what's working and what's not working, make improvements to the business, and develop the people. In short, the leader needs to work ON the business, not just IN the business.

A good leader leads the people from above them.
A great leader leads the people from within them.
–M. D. Arnold

A good leader inspires people to have confidence in their leader.
A great leader inspires people to have confidence in themselves.
–author unknown

2
SIMPLE BUT HARD

We often hear people say dismissively that leadership is really nothing more than common sense. This implies that leadership is easy, and anyone can be a successful leader.

Our response to that is, "Poppycock!" (We're not quite sure what poppycock means, but it makes us feel British to say it, and for some reason, that feels good.)

Leadership may be common sense, but it certainly isn't common practice. The reason it's not common practice is because IT'S HARD!

Leadership requires reading a situation, considering the players involved, and figuring out how to respond constructively. Leadership takes massive amounts of skill and flexibility.

Leaders constantly...
- make themselves available to other people
- rely on and support other people
- listen to other people
- stay calm when other people are upset
- remain upbeat when other people are down
- have tough conversations with people
- make decisions when there are no clear answers

This takes an abundance of patience and self-control, and it is exhausting! Leadership is not a sprint; it's a marathon.

The challenge with leadership is not the *knowing*; it's the *doing*. It's having the energy and the discipline to consistently execute the vision well.

So for all of you out there struggling to be better leaders, don't give up. It's a tough gig, but it's worth the struggle.

Here's a quick leadership story before we move on to the next chapter:

I was a twenty-three year old Ensign on my first Navy ship, where I found myself in charge of a division of 19 men, 15 of whom were older than me. After being on board for just two weeks, I was called to attend my first Captain's Mast (disciplinary board) for one of the enlisted sailors in my division for a disorderly conduct charge.

The man was in his 30's, had tattoos on each arm, and looked like one tough customer. I stood there in front of our Captain as he read the charges, which included bad behavior fueled by a night of too much alcohol. When the Captain asked what punishment I would recommend, I could have pleaded ignorance, since I had not been on the ship when the incident occurred, or I could have just told the captain that the sailor should receive an appropriate punishment for an incident of this nature.

Instead, I told him I felt the man in question understood his offense and he would not let it happen again. The captain agreed to drop the charge, but made it clear that he did not want to see him at Captain's Mast again. Later that evening, the petty officer asked why I had defended him since I didn't even know him. I told him that I felt he deserved another chance, but that if he were to go to Captain's Mast again, I would ask for the maximum punishment. He agreed and thanked me for standing up for him.

Here are two things I learned:

1. I could have been the cool new officer and sent a message that I would not tolerate misbehavior by requesting the maximum punishment. I'm not sure how that would have worked out for me in the long term with the crew, but I barely knew my team at this point, so I felt I needed to give him the benefit of the doubt before passing judgement. The IRON FIST type leadership was not my style.
2. I later found out that the petty officer was well respected among the division, and he let them know that I was going to be fair with them. Your team can make you successful or they can make you a failure. Because of the way I handled my first disciplinary encounter, my team made me very successful during my time on the ship.

A leader should always work to remain calm and upbeat in order to build a relationship with his or her team or division.

3
COME UP WITH A GOAL

One of the principles good leaders need to understand is that people really do want to make a difference at work. People want to have an impact. People want to be part of something successful. So a good leader needs to provide the team with a plan of action or goal. (Note: We were tempted to use the term "vision" instead of "goal," but visioning is lofty CEO work, and most of our readers won't be CEO's. So we went with "goal.")

A goal is an aspiration for the team. It's what the company or division or department can accomplish if everyone pitches in to make it happen. A goal is what gives people focus and direction. A goal is what gives people the energy to hang in there when things start to feel like a grind. Without goals, your team members start to sound like the Cat in *Alice in Wonderland*:

> *"Would you tell me, please, which way I ought to go from here?" said Alice.*
> *"That depends a good deal on where you want to get to," said the Cat.*
> *"I don't much care where," said Alice.*
> *"Then it doesn't matter which way you go," said the Cat.*

Or even worse, they start to sound like Yogi Berra:

> *If you don't know where you are going,*
> *you'll end up someplace else.*
> *—Yogi Berra*

Or worse yet, they start to sound like the burned out guy from *Office Space*:

> *The thing is, Bob, it's not that I'm lazy, it's that I just don't care.*
> *—Peter Gibbons*

A quick story on goals:

Our ship was leaving on New Year's Eve for a six-month deployment. As you can imagine, no one was very happy about leaving in the middle of the holidays, but duty called.

One of my jobs as an officer was to stand watch on the bridge. While I stood watch one day, the Captain asked about my goals for the deployment.

Not feeling particularly excited about leaving my new bride, I told him I would be happy just to survive the six months until we returned home.

Evidently that wasn't the answer he was looking for, as he made it loud and clear that simply surviving was no goal and that I needed to get my head in the game. I was taken aback by the quick backlash. Our ship had just won the best ship award and we had a great crew, so I was wondering what the big deal was. What I didn't realize at the time is that the Captain saw a lot of potential in me and felt I should have my goals for the deployment mapped out. After the tongue lashing by the Captain that day, I set out to build a set of goals for the next six months, not only for me, but for my division. Meeting these goals contributed to the overall success of the ship's mission, resulting in another best ship award.

Don't Underestimate the Power of Goals!

4
MAKE SURE THE GOAL RESONATES

The goal needs to get people excited. It needs to be something people want to embrace. It needs to be something that speaks to people personally.

The sad truth about goals is that they tend to be incremental performance measures that aren't personal enough to inspire anyone. "Grow sales by 30%" or "reduce costs by 5%" doesn't really speak to people's souls.

And don't get us started on meaningless vision statements: "Our vision is to be the premier, unparalleled, world class, best-in-class, most respected, most admired company in our industry." Puh-lease!

The leader needs to find the sweet spot within the goal – not too big and not too small – and make it interesting to the team. Consider things like:

- Being the top-ranked team in the company
- Winning *Vendor of the Year* from our biggest customer
- Reducing our backlog, so people don't have to work overtime

A common mistake is setting a goal that doesn't feel realistic or achievable to the team. When that happens, the team loses interest immediately, and the odds of success plummet. To make the goal more than wallpaper, it has to resonate with them.

Make sure each person on the team understands how his or her job impacts team success. Remember, people want to feel important and want to contribute something meaningful. Everyone's contribution is important, no matter what their job is in the company.

As a leader it is up to you to promote the goal on a daily basis and develop a realistic urgency as you head toward it.

If you have to adjust the plan along the way, that is perfectly acceptable. Communication as you are adjusting is the key to getting continued support from positions above and below you in your journey.

Things to consider when setting a goal:

- The complexity of the product line.
- The speed of product and technology changes in the industry.
- The amount of support infrastructure in place to support the rapidly changing environment.
- The ability to get investments to improve technology and hire staff to support the business. You will need to convince the senior leaders that the investment will pay off.

These items are important because you have to consider what you can control with your team and what may need investment dollars or resources outside of your control. It is critical to identify these four items up front so you can accurately establish the goal to create success. As noted previously, stay vigilant with your goals and create an urgency for getting them done.

One of the most common mistakes leaders make is that they create lofty goals that don't align with the company strategy, require outside resources to accomplish, or require major capital investment. Goals of this nature quickly become wallpaper, or become a finger pointing exercise as to why they were not accomplished.

You may have heard of SMART goals:

S – Specific
M – Measurable
A – Achievable
R – Results Oriented
T – Time Bound

Using the SMART goal framework will give you a quick guide to creating impactful goals for your teams. Many teams make twelve-month goals all ending in December, but we would recommend staggering the time frames, so you can celebrate success on a regular basis.

5
INSIST ON A PLAN

Goals are great, but there needs to be a game plan to achieve the goal, otherwise the goal is just wishful thinking.

> *Hope is not a strategy.*
> *—author unknown*

> *Vision without execution is hallucination.*
> *—Thomas Edison*

The plan must be real – it needs to involve clear commitments, and it needs to involve some tough choices about doing things differently, changing focus, and reallocating resources. You can't just add additional priorities to peoples' already busy schedules and expect good things to happen.

> *The definition of insanity is doing the same thing over and over again*
> *and expecting different results.*
> *—Albert Einstein*

You should continuously stress the need for a plan to your teams. A good rule of thumb is one-third planning and two-thirds execution.

Guard against Paralysis through Analysis!!

6
LET YOUR TEAM MEMBERS DRIVE THE PLAN

It is the leader's job to make sure there is a plan. It is not the leader's job to single-handedly build the plan.

In fact, there are two very powerful reasons why leaders should heavily involve their team in the development of the plan: know-how and commitment.

The people doing the work know the most about it, hands down. Some leaders think it makes them look uninformed or weak to ask for input from their team members. But the truth is, it makes leaders look wise and humble to ask for input from their team. Leaders don't need to have all the answers; they just need to know what to ask of the right people.

The ones doing the work need to be committed to the plan. No commitment means no execution. The best way to get people committed to the plan is to let them develop the plan. You can still participate in the planning process – you don't have to take your hands off the steering wheel completely – but the plan needs to belong to the team.

> *People who plan the battle rarely battle the plan.*
> *—author unknown*

> *The answer you give is never as good as the one they find.*
> *—author unknown*

Leadership is a team sport. You can't win by yourself. If you don't like people, or don't like dealing with people's issues, or don't have patience, then don't take a leadership position.

> *If you want to go fast, go alone.*
> *If you want to go far, go together.*
> *--African proverb*

9

7
PROGRESS OVER PERFECTION

The plan doesn't need to be perfect. In fact, there is no such thing as a perfect plan – there are too many unknowns and too many moving parts. Be willing to modify the plan as you go. Ownership is more important than perfection. Progress is more important than perfection. Forward progress and small wins are the main objectives.

> *No battle plan survives initial contact with the enemy.*
> *–Helmuth von Moltke*

> *A good plan executed now is better than a perfect plan executed next week.*
> *–George Patton*

Leaders often want a project to be perfect before officially launching it. This can create major delays in providing programs that your customers need right now. It's important to realize that most projects will never be perfect. Follow your project plan and get customer feedback along the way, so you can satisfy customer expectations. Some of your projects will be hits right out of the gate, requiring only minor tweaks to get them up to full speed. However, many projects will need significant adjustments after launch. Don't see this as a failure and become discouraged; rather, see this as another route to success.

A key decision is to determine when to pull the trigger on the product launch. If you assemble the right team, you can be confident that you will hit the target when the time comes to launch your project. If you never pull the trigger, you will always fail to hit the target.

If you are leading a project, make sure you have regular and recurring meetings with the team to get their input. This will bring to the surface any concerns or potential challenges to the project. Make it clear that each team member should raise issues early and not let them linger. This will ensure you will not face unnecessary delays or launch a product that may potentially miss the mark.

Things to keep in mind when leading a project team.

- As the leader, know what behaviors you want, and communicate them to the team – a code of conduct, if you

10

will.

- Display these behaviors yourself. Be the example.
- Make these behaviors part of the team routine so they stay visible and part of your success.

Here are two examples of projects I led that would have missed the target had we not released them when we did.

Project 1

Our company was working on a software maintenance upgrade program. With about two weeks until the release date, the team held a meeting and hit a roadblock. After listening for a few minutes, I asked if any of the roadblocks were show stoppers. Everyone agreed that none of them were, so I asked each person their greatest concern. As we went around the table, we addressed each question and found a workable solution for each item.

We made all the changes and updates we needed to get the project launched on time. Though this project was not an instant success at launch, it became a very valuable product to our customers after just a few tweaks. Had we waited to launch, we would have jeopardized a year's worth of revenue because a few team members got nervous that the project wasn't going to be perfect.

Project 2

Another project involved a major revamp of our customer web portal that provided knowledge based articles to our customers. My goal was to have this project up and running in twelve months. The team thought it was doable, so we kicked the project off.

After challenges with web developers, finding database managers and other tedious things, we passed the twelve-month mark with no web portal release. Though the team continued to resolve one challenge after another, we felt it would take another six months to ensure all the critical elements were included.

When this new deadline was upon us, about half the team felt like we were ready, and the other half wanted to wait another month. We launched the project.

Although we had a few glitches upon launch, none were out of the ordinary for a project of this magnitude, and the site turned out to be a huge success.

Lessons I Learned:

1. As the leader you need to thoroughly evaluate whether delays are warranted or just nerves. It is your job to bring calm to the team to get at the root of any issue so you can put a plan together to get it resolved.
2. Don't be afraid to adjust the project after launch. Major items should not be missed, but it's normal for minor issues to surface. These can be addressed as they occur.
3. It is wise to scope the project properly in the pre-planning stage. This will uncover challenges that you may not have thought about initially.
4. Trust your team and meet frequently to review the project, so serious challenges can be dealt with early.
5. Trust your team, but ultimately you have to make the decision to push the go button and take accountability.

8
RELATIONSHIPS FIRST

Leaders tend to be action-oriented. They want to get things done. They see problems, and they want to tell people how to fix them.

Unfortunately, most people don't want to be told how to fix things, unless they've asked for the help. This aversion to input and advice is particularly strong in people who have done a job for a long time, take great pride in what they do, and identify strongly with what they do. They feel like experts, and want to be treated like experts. To these people, input and advice feels disrespectful, especially if such direction comes from a new leader. This is when you hear comments like, "I've been doing this job since you were in diapers."

Before employees will accept input and advice from their leader, they need to trust their leader. They want to know the leader respects them, and they want to know the leader has their back. So focus first on building a relationship with your people before you start imparting your wisdom on them.

> *People don't care how much you know until they know how much you care.*
> *—Theodore Roosevelt*

Leaders often ask their teams to take a leap of faith when things are tough. Working closely with your team and making them part of the plan before times get stressful will inspire them to take that leap and keep going during the difficult times.

When the going gets tough, leaders who have already demonstrated genuine concern for team members and have built relationships are more likely to inspire the team to rise to the occasion. During trying times, leaders must often ask teams to make sacrifices for the company. It is the leader's respect and genuine concern for the team that makes team members support tough decisions and push forward during these difficult times.

9
BUILD YOUR CREDITS

At some point as a leader, you'll need to have tough conversations with your team members. You will have to tell them they're doing something incorrectly or you'll have to ask them to do something they don't want to do. At some point, you'll have to make withdrawals from your relationship account.

Your goal should be to have a strong enough relationship with your team members to withstand those tough conversations. So make plenty of deposits to your relationship account. Have lots of positive conversations with people before you have the negative ones.

- Spend time getting to know your group and letting them get to know you, so they are comfortable with you and trust you.
- Spend time asking for their opinions and input.
- Spend time recognizing and thanking them for their hard work.
- Spend time asking what they need from you to make them more efficient and successful.

When people are treated with respect and praised for their contributions, they are much more likely to accept constructive guidance.

I read a quote the other day that went something like this – "When I talk to managers they make me feel like *they* are important! When I talk to leaders they make me feel like *I* am important." You would be surprised at how quickly team members can feel the difference.

Positive reinforcement sounds like an easy one, but it is amazing how many leaders miss the mark. The challenge here is to be consistent and authentic about praise (it's easy to sniff out a phony). However, guard against the appearance that there are favorites within the teams you lead.

Here are few examples of what *not* to do.

1. I once worked for a fireplace manufacturer, and since my department supported them, I wanted to know how the fireplaces were built. The easiest way to gain this information was to tag along on the morning walk through the plant with the plant manager. We would stop at different stations to get the status of

14

daily production. When the production numbers were not met, the plant manager publicly chastised his team members in front of the whole group. Production never improved while he was the plant manager.

2. I worked with a senior director of product marketing who was responsible for new product initiatives. Monthly calls were held with upwards of 20 to 30 people to review all the new product introductions. He would interrupt his people while they were presenting and scream, demean, and berate them. In some instances, others on the phone would ask to get back on topic and request to move on, just to stop the verbal abuse. This individual would also get mad in group meetings and storm out of the meeting right in front of his boss.

Both scenarios are the exact opposite of relentless encouragement or leadership. These "leaders" led by intimidation and not with respect for their team members. Leaders have to remember to praise employees in public and correct them in private. Notice I said correct, not chastise. Behavior like this is definitely not the sign of a good leader.

Now on to a more positive example:

My team and I were developing a new software maintenance upgrade package to sell our customers, who, in turn could buy the upgraded package at a fraction of the cost of our next software revision package. It was a chance for customers to lock in early and save money.

We put together a sales campaign and offered our sales team an incentive program to gain extra commission for the sale of each new upgrade package. At the end of the predetermined sales period, I met with the inside sales manager to ask how we had done with the new product sales incentive program. Disheartened, she admitted they had sold just two units. Undeterred, I suggested the sales team should continue to offer the product upgrade.

As the months went by, sales started picking up because customers were starting to realize the huge benefit of locking in early with our upgrade package. In just one year, we were selling over $15,000 per month.

Had I not provided the encouragement to our inside sales team early, they would have stopped selling this new product and missed a great revenue opportunity. Furthermore, we would have denied our customers an opportunity to save money over the long term with our products.

Remember that sometimes it takes a little while to get traction with new ideas or projects.

As the leader, you need to be the head cheerleader. I always tell my teams to remain positive if a coworker is being negative. It is easy to get pulled into negativity, but it is so counterproductive. If someone on the team needs some more positive reinforcement, it is a good idea to enlist in other teammates to help them maintain a positive work environment.

When things go wrong, find ways to make improvements rather than dwelling on the negative. Find and promote the positive in an otherwise negative situation. Your teams will appreciate it and look to you to be the spark when the going gets tough. Being the person who consistently promotes the notion of "the glass half full," will reap unintended consequences; the organization's culture will change over time, with more employees becoming cheerleaders when times get tough. This strategy builds a very loyal workforce, and your customers will benefit from a great experience time and time again, as happy employees will deliver exceptional customer service.

10
MOTIVATION IS KEY

In case you haven't picked up on this already, leaders need to be obsessed with building their team's motivation. Broadly speaking, there are two big factors that drive performance: ability and motivation. And with most jobs, motivation is a much bigger deal than ability.

So, when we tell you to make sure the goal resonates, involve people in planning, let people own the plan, and build relationships with people, we're really talking about building motivation.

Remember, first and foremost, you want people to care about what they're doing. If people have pride and a sense of purpose, they will push through the tough times, and won't let petty stuff knock them off course.

As a leader, your litmus test for every interaction you have with your team should be, "How is this interaction going to affect their motivation?" Even if you have to deliver bad news, you need to do it in a way that doesn't kill motivation.

> *More mistakes at work are made by those who do not care*
> *than by those who do not know.*
> *--author unknown*

You want team members to work carefully. You want people to create and follow standard operating procedures. You don't want people to take shortcuts.

You want team members to work together. You want them to communicate and coordinate within their immediate team and across teams, so everyone is pulling in the same direction. You don't want people to think only about their own piece of the puzzle.

You want team members to speak their mind. Be open to their ideas and opinions for making things better, faster, and cheaper. To quote authors Adrian Gostick and Chester Elton, "You have employees walking around with brilliant ideas in their pockets. You need to get them to empty their pockets."

You want team members to ask for help. You want team members actively engaged in professional development, rather than actively engaged in hiding their weaknesses.

You want team members to take initiative. Empower them to make decisions and resolve issues in real time.

All of these positive behaviors boil down to motivation. When the engagement factor is high, good things happen!

11
PROVIDE TOP COVER

One way to build a relationship with your team is to protect them from outside threats.

- If someone criticizes your team, you should take the hit on behalf of the team, then make internal adjustments as needed.
- If someone makes unreasonable demands on your team, you need to step in and deal with it.
- Don't let your teams be burdened with activities that should be handled by another team. Your team members will appreciate your support.
- If your team needs cooperation from outside groups, you need to work to make that happen.
- If your team thinks you're only worried about yourself, they won't give you their best work.

It is extremely important to understand your core responsibilities. This allows you to quickly identify non-core requirements that need to be dealt with and eliminated. It is the leader's job to be the gatekeeper in order to keep unwanted activities and attitudes out of your department.

12
HOLD PEOPLE ACCOUNTABLE

Accountability
- is about keeping score at an individual level.
- is about pulling your weight.
- is about doing what you say you're going to do.
- is about striving for both individual and team excellence.
- is about personal responsibility.

Holding people accountable is about helping people be successful.

Achieving accountability means developing clear expectations with your team members, getting clear commitments from team members, and then having ongoing, real and direct conversations about team member performance.

Accountability can lead to uncomfortable discussions with people who are underperforming. But those discussions are absolutely critical to the success of the team, so it's incumbent on the leader to have those discussions.

Instilling a culture of accountability is ultimately how you win as a team.

13
ENGAGE WITH YOUR TEAM

Stay visible. If your team can't see you, they'll wonder what you're doing.

This expectation might sound easy, but time and time again I see leaders who don't spend enough time with their teams. No matter how much you think they already know, your team is interested in what is happening with the department, company, and industry. Remember and practice the basics. Communication is key!

My early experience with the Navy drove home the importance of communication. While stationed on a ship, we assembled our department every morning to distribute information from the Captain. We would pass along events of the day, any scheduled drills, and any other necessary information to the department.

Here are some ways to reinforce communication when leading a team:

1. Set up regular team meetings to discuss what is going on within the department as well as in the company. You will be amazed at how much people don't know about what is going on outside their own department.
2. Ask your team for monthly input on successes they have had for the month. Success comes in many sizes, and you need to recognize them all.
3. Meet with your teams to discuss good things as well as challenges. People tend to expect bad news when a meeting is called. Break that trend. If you plan to discuss a positive item, do not discuss negative issues during the same meeting. Instead call another meeting for that discussion. It is not always possible to hold two meetings, but try to avoid following good news with bad news.
4. Walk around the department and sincerely ask people how they are doing. People will appreciate the fact that you get out of your office and have an interest in their work.

There are many things you can do to engage with your team members. Pick the items that work for you and fit your style. You need to be comfortable engaging your team members or your teams will feel that you're just going through the motions and don't really care about them.

21

14
ENCOURAGE REFLECTION

Good leaders strive to improve their processes and their methods of doing business to give customers what they need and desire. Great leaders support team members who want to innovate, and create the flexibility to make innovation successful.

When I started a new job managing a large call center, I held introductory meetings with each team. Here are a few things I learned:

- Communication between groups was low and there was no incentive to work outside the team unless absolutely necessary.
- There was no local senior leadership in the building that spent significant time developing these teams on a regular basis.
- Team member development was low, and many team members were in a rut just trying to get through the day.
- The customer and support services were not well understood; hence, they did not have a voice in how they could assist the corporation's success.
- The technical support teams had just implemented a new Customer Relationship Management (CRM) system and there were negative or perceived negative issues with the new system.
- They had few metrics that were measured each month and no action items.

Here's what I did to get things moving forward:

- Created and communicated goals for the teams, so they had a vision of where we were going.
- Worked to create collaborative projects to get the groups working together. Continuous improvement and innovation were at the forefront of these projects.
- Held quarterly meetings to communicate the team's successes.
- Started addressing low performers. We worked to turn them around or help them find new employment. I made it clear that we needed to change to improve.
- I tackled the new CRM system that the team members thought was worse than the old one. A quick way to get credibility with your teams is by tackling the pain points early. We discovered it

was not the CRM system after all; it was the network capacity of the facility. We worked to upgrade the network, and the system improved immensely.

A short time later:

- In addition to multiple awards for our individual team members, our team was recognized by our business unit as being the best Customer & Product Support team in the business group.
- Lower performers were addressed, and the team became much stronger.
- The team focused on core responsibilities.
- Team metrics improved significantly, and our voice of the customer surveys improved dramatically.
- Team member innovation ideas continued to drive productivity that improved the customer experience.

The success I had at that position could not have been possible had I not listened to my team members. I made it clear to the team leaders that I was committed to their success. I wanted to learn about their departments, not micromanage them. I wanted to understand the road blocks, so I could help remove them. It is very important that your team members know you support their drive to succeed.

15
BUILD PROCESSES TO SUSTAIN IMPROVEMENTS

Process development is critical to sustainability of the business, as it drives efficiency and productivity. There are three key elements to process development:

1. Map the process for the first time and test it to make sure you have captured the process from beginning to end.
2. Revisit the process on a regular basis to ensure it hasn't changed.
3. Identify waste in the process to eliminate it. This will ensure that your teams are driving consistency within a particular activity, that they are efficient and that the process is current.

Leaders need to demonstrate the value of process creation. Easy, you say? Not always. If you have long-term team members who are the "so-called" experts, it may take some convincing for them to share their knowledge. Remember, knowledge feels like power to many people, so they hoard it.

Remember to be constructive when you discuss a process that a group has developed. Start by asking your team what processes they have and how often they review them. A mature team will be able to tell you these answers quickly and be able to show you their process documentation. If you are dealing with a mature group, you can then start asking how they review processes or what their current challenges are. This will point to areas for process review and lead to opportunities for improvement. No matter how efficient a team is, they can always find improvements.

If your teams are new or do not have many processes, you will want to start with what the team feels are the critical issues. The trick is not to try to fix everything at once. Look for the low effort/high impact projects to get quick wins, and then recognize the team's success. Involve your team members, because they will have ideas of where to start. This is an opportunity to have your team members speak their minds and offer suggestions.

Building processes is a great opportunity to work together toward a common goal. Don't always pick your best people to lead the projects. Involve different people as you work your way from one process to the next. Get everyone involved in one way or another to spread the knowledge around. Open up cross departmental processes to drive cross functional teamwork. You will be amazed at the results.

One of the first successes I had with my teams was reviewing a process in which customers had a significant wait to obtain authorization to replace a certain piece of equipment The process did work, but it took 21 days and three different people to complete the shipment. No one perceived this as a problem, even though another process for equipment replacements existed that only took 24 hours. What would our customer think when they could get most things shipped in 24 hours, but if they needed this particular piece of equipment they waited 3 weeks? I saw this service gap as a big opportunity for process improvement. A team reviewed the process and discovered that the 24-hour process could be replicated for this product. Think of the time saved and the waste eliminated. Our customers were thrilled, and the team was astonished at the results and was excited to take on the next process.

Just tweaking a process made our team much more productive and able to take on additional customer support duties without increasing our staffing. Most importantly, our customers benefited from our process improvements.

16
TAKE YOUR OWN MEDICINE

Leaders spend a significant amount of time encouraging team members to be open to feedback, coaching, and help. Guess what? Leaders need to make the same accommodations for themselves.

Leaders, like team members, should always have a mentor or someone they have worked for in the past whom they can lean on in times of uncertainty or turmoil. Leaders are not invincible, so be cautious around anyone who thinks they are.

Some people have a hard time accepting advice or guidance. They think that if they ask for or accept help, they are showing weakness or lack of expertise. In reality, raising a hand to get input shows strength and integrity, and usually results in a better decision for the team.

I routinely encourage my team members to ask questions if they need help, so I need to be willing to do the same thing. If you have a peer that you work closely with, he or she can be a great resource. Since this person may not be an expert on your topic, they will likely ask questions to better understand the situation. This tends to bring out solutions as you talk through the challenge.

Have you ever had a team member look you in the eye and tell you that you should do what you tell them to do? (Also known as practice what you preach?) I have. There are two ways to react to this feedback. You can react with anger, thinking the team member is disrespecting your position, or you can reflect on what the team member said because it may be true. You may just need to start following your own advice.

Have you ever taken a 360 evaluation? It's an evaluation that can be quite eye opening. You not only evaluate yourself, but you ask peers, subordinates, and your superiors to evaluate you. It's a complete circle of feedback – that's why it's called 360, for 360 degrees.

I took my first 360 evaluation during my first leadership position. I felt I was pretty good at a number of things and did not see many weaknesses in my leadership style. Certainly, I always had room to learn, but I was confident that things were going well in my group and the business.

26

When I received the results of the evaluation, I was very surprised with the grades I received in a number of areas. It was hard listening to my team members describe areas where I needed to improve. It was also tough to hear feedback without getting defensive, but I did my best to be open to each suggestion. This experience was invaluable in shaping my leadership skills over the years. I took their advice to heart and made changes and adjusted my leadership style. My team members appreciated the opportunity to give me feedback and the respect I had for their input.

Another situation when I realized I needed to take my own medicine was when my company went through a leadership shake up. Many of the old guard were being fired and the new team was coming in and making no secret that things were going to change. I was the Director of Customer Service and I heard that the effectiveness of our department was in question. In interactions with my teams, I stayed positive and asked them to do the same. With my peers and close colleagues, I expressed concern and wondered whether it was worth staying on at the risk of being fired.

Word got back to my boss that I was not happy and had a bad attitude. Later that week, my boss challenged me to either get in the game or step aside, because my attitude was not acceptable. I had great respect for my boss, and I told her I would get my attitude straight. Although I didn't appreciate it at the time, I'm glad I was confronted, because I needed to heed my own advice.

A leader who is open to continuous learning and input from above, below, and beside will drive loyalty for the business. Leaders need to evaluate and evolve their skill sets as often as they ask their teams to evaluate theirs, because business continues to change. Continuous learning will give you a competitive advantage over your competition.

17
ADMIT WHEN YOU'RE WRONG

Many leaders believe it is a sign of weakness to admit mistakes. I think that there is strength in being willing to take responsibility for something that has gone wrong. I have heard many whispers from team members when the leader won't take ownership, or even worse, starts pointing fingers at others when things don't go as planned.

An example of this was an incident I ran into while in the boating industry. Customers were complaining that the boat covers we made to fit our boats did not fit correctly. So after modifying the covers, we thought our issue was resolved. Shortly thereafter, I visited a customer site and was greeted by a frustrated manager. We had sent him a cover that did not fit the boat correctly and then denied his warranty claim.

I told him I could resolve the problem and spent the next 20 minutes unsuccessfully trying to correct the issue. Sheepishly, I admitted he was right and made the immediate decision to cover the cost of the repair. The customer was happy because he knew I was being fair by covering the product under warranty.

Another example of a time when I had to take ownership of a poor decision is when I hired the wrong person for a job. I corrected the situation by terminating the bad hire, but I owned up to the mistake. I didn't attempt to blame my team or anyone else. When leaders make a bad decision, they need to take responsibility for it, fix it, and learn from it.

18
ADAPT TO THE CHANGING COMPETITIVE LANDSCAPE

Technology and business practices are changing at lightning speed. In order to stay competitive, you need to be vigilant to changing trends and adjust along the way. Otherwise, you may find out the hard way that you are lagging behind when a competitor offers a new service or product.

All parts of the business are susceptible to changing times. Let's take a look at it from the support side. Your customers continue to look for ways that they can increase their efficiency and productivity to grow their business and increase profitability. They are looking to their manufacturers to assist on this front.

Customers are looking for self-help options and also data analytics to optimize their businesses. With the changing demographics of the workforce, online solutions continue to grow. The challenge with online help is that it has to be user friendly or it will not be fully utilized. Before you put a bunch of information out there, get feedback from your customer as to what information they want to see. At the very least, try to hold a focus group to get information from your customers. This will be invaluable in setting up self-help tools.

So what does this mean for your internal teams? You may have to create positions that don't currently exist in your organization. You may need to add resources to drive online initiatives. Here are some items customers consistently look for online:

1. Frequently Asked Questions (FAQ's)
2. User manuals
3. Short self-help videos
4. Technical bulletins or policy revisions
5. Contact numbers for your company

Monitor your website to see the number of visits you are receiving and what pages your customers are accessing the most. The benefit of gathering this data is that you can feed it back to your Engineering and Quality teams to work to improve your website information.

Collecting data is great, but what do you do with it?

I had to address a dilemma a few years ago. Our corporate customers wanted reports detailing how often and why their technicians were contacting us for help. After unsuccessfully trying to utilize our already busy technicians, we created a dedicated data analyst position. The analyst was able provide the requested information in a timely manner.

Our decision to create this position succeeded. Our customers received reports that were easy to understand and provided them with valuable information. We then automated the reporting to our web portal, which made access to the reports even easier for our clients. Updates were done in real time with minimal maintenance on our side.

Keep an eye on trends so you don't get caught lagging behind. Remember, strive to create value for your customers. It will increase their loyalty for your products. Sales is a big part of this success, but support is a valued contributor as well.

19
LEADERS NEED TO RECHARGE TOO!

Leading teams is no easy task. You have to be on point all the time. Your team is continuously watching to see if you are going to take charge or fail. Leaders above you are evaluating your skills to see if you are a good fit for their teams. There is a great deal of pressure to be successful.

Our lives have become so busy with meetings and requests from all directions that many times we lose sight of our purpose. There's a great quote that says, "People don't burn out because of what they do; they burn out because they forget why they do it." Leaders need to take time to recharge so they can hit the next challenge fully engaged. How do you do that, you ask?

There are many ways to find a little time for yourself. We're not talking about major vacations or trips to the spa (though both of these are nice). We're talking about intentionally carving out moments within your day to recharge and reflect. Here are a few ideas for creating time during your day:

1. Disconnect during your commute. Don't listen to podcasts or check your email – just embrace the time to think.
2. Take a 10-minute walk during the day, and don't take your phone with you. The office can survive without you for 10 minutes.
3. If you've got an office, shut the door for 10 minutes, and give yourself a chance to do some uninterrupted thinking.
4. When you travel, take a little time on planes or in taxis to think about your teams and your business.

The point is that leaders need time to clear their minds in order to guide their teams to new heights. Leaders need to rise above the minutia to drive strategy and vision.

Find the method that works best for you, but make sure it becomes part of your regular routine. You need this time to refresh your mind, reduce the chance of burnout, and keep your mind in the game.

Find your Mindfulness.
It really will make a difference.

20
WRAP UP

We have given you many things to consider on your journey to becoming a better leader. Being a successful leader is not about being the most liked or the flashiest person in the room. It is about doing the little things for your team members and the teams around you, while bringing value to your customers. It is about recognizing great performance, communicating on a regular basis, and sharing your vision with the team. It is about creating environments where people want to contribute and be successful.

There are mentors and coaches along the way who can help you, but ultimately it is up to you to create your own path to success.

Good Luck and Find Success!!

ABOUT THE AUTHORS

Ray Roberge is a Customer Service professional who has led "World Class" contact centers and has been recognized for creating first class customer service, warranty and technical support teams for a number of Fortune 100 companies.

He holds an MBA from The University of Tennessee Haslam College of Business and has more than 20 years of Customer Service experience in multiple industries.

Dr. Michael McIntyre leads the Executive MBA for Strategic Leadership in the Haslam College of Business at The University of Tennessee. He also works with companies all over the country in the areas of leadership and culture. He earned his PhD in Industrial-Organizational Psychology from The University of Tennessee, and his BS in Policy Analysis from Cornell University.

Made in the USA
Lexington, KY
19 April 2018